Fun-to-Knit
Doll Clothes™

Designs by Andra Knight-Bowman

HOUSE of
WHITE
BIRCHES

PUBLISHERS
SINCE 1947

Table of Contents

Summertime Susie,
page 4

Nighttime Nicole,
page 26

Nautical Nancy,
page 7

Casual Caitlyn,
page 12

Evening-Wear Ella,
page 18

Jogging Josie,
page 21

Rah-Rah Rachel,
page 31

Introduction

The 18-inch doll has been an American favorite for many years. So why shouldn't she have some cute and cozy hand-knitted outfits for all seasons? Make them for your grandchild, child or even to bring out the child in you. After all, who didn't love to dress dolls in new clothes?

We all know how tedious knitting small items can be, especially for dolls due to their body shaping. So please, enjoy the friendly knitting outfits that I have designed that do not need usually-required snaps or hook-and-eye closures.

I've had the most fun creating these designs. After all, this is how my designing career started, making sweaters for my own dolls at a very young age.

Andra Knight-Bowman

Meet The Designer

At the age of 7, I learned to knit, and I was a natural at the craft. I soon started making sweaters for my Barbie dolls and my dog, Mitzi. Designing entered my life at an early age.

In high school, I had the opportunity to work at a local yarn shop; it was there I learned about fibers and sweater designing. My goal in life was to own a yarn shop of my own.

I opened Knits & Pearls in 2004 and introduced many of my designs from previous years to my customers. Since then I have created many more designs. They have been published in numerous magazines and a book titled *Easy Cable Knits for all Seasons*. I feel so blessed and am grateful for everyone who has believed in me.

PHOTO BY GREG SEAVER

I reside in Johnson City, Tenn., with my wonderful husband, Terry, who has been a gem through book writings and two furry kids (cats), Billie and Blue. I just couldn't ask for a better life!

House of White Birches, Berne, Indiana 46711   DRGnetwork.com

Summertime Susie

Designs by Andra Knight-Bowman

Skill Level

 INTERMEDIATE

Finished Measurements

Chest: 11 inches
Length: 7½ inches

Materials

- Plymouth Jeannee Worsted (worsted weight; 51% cotton/49% acrylic; 110 yds/50g per ball): 4 balls pastel variegated #100
- Size 6 (4mm) needles
- Size 7 (4.5mm) needles or size needed to obtain gauge
- Cable needle
- Stitch holder
- Tapestry needle

Gauge

20 sts and 28 rows = 4 inches/10cm in St st with larger needles.
To save time, take time to check gauge.

Special Abbreviation

Make 1 (M1): Insert LH needle from front to back into strand between st just worked and next st, k1-tbl.

Dress

Back/Front

Make 2

With smaller needle, cast on 56 sts. Knit 3 rows.

Change to larger needles and work in St st until piece measures 5 inches, ending with a WS row.

Next row: [Sl next 2 sts onto cn, hold in back, knit next 2 sts, one at a time tog with sts on cn] 7 times, [sl next 2 sts onto cn, hold in front, knit next 2 sts, one at a time tog with sts on cn] 7 times—28 sts.

Knit 3 rows.

Beg with RS row work in St st until piece measures 7¼ inches, ending with a RS row.

Knit 3 rows. Bind off loosely.

Straps

Make 2

With larger needles, cast on 4 sts. Work in garter st for 4 inches. Bind off loosely.

Bow

With larger needles, cast on 4 sts. Work in garter st for 18 inches. Bind off loosely. Tie in bow.

Assembly

Sew side seams. Sew straps to front and back 1¼ inches in from each side seam. Attach bow to center of back at waist.

Hat

Crown

Beg at lower edge of crown, with larger needles, cast on 58 sts. Work in St st for 6 rows.

Row 1 (dec row): K1, [k6, k2tog] 7times, end k1—51 sts.

Row 2 and all even-numbered rows: Purl.

Row 3: K1, [k5, k2tog] 7 times, end k1—44 sts.

Row 5: K1, [k4, k2tog] 7 times, end k1—37 sts.

Row 7: K1, [k3, k2tog] 7 times, end k1—30 sts.

Row 9: K1, [k2, k2tog] 7 times, end k1—23 sts.

Row 11: K1, [k1, k2tog] 7 times, end k1—16 sts.

Row 13: K1, [k2tog] 7 times, end k1—9 sts.

Cut yarn leaving 6-inch tail. Place sts on holder.

Brim

With RS facing and larger needles, pick up 57 sts along cast on edge of crown. Knit 1 row.

Next row (RS): *K3, M1; rep from * to last 3 sts, k3—75 sts.

Knit 3 rows.

Next row: K1, *M1, k3; rep from * to last 2 sts, M1, k2—100 sts.

Knit 3 rows.

Next row: *K3, M1; rep from * to last st, k1—134 sts.

Knit 3 rows. Bind off loosely.

Assembly

Thread yarn from crown on tapestry needle, pulling tightly through sts on holder. Sew seam. ❖

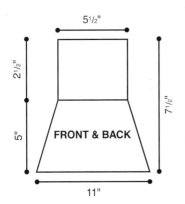

Nautical Nancy

Designs by Andra Knight-Bowman

Skill Level

■■■□ INTERMEDIATE

Finished measurements

Chest: 14 inches
Sweater Length: 6½ inches
Shorts Length: 6 inches

Materials

- Plymouth Galway Worsted (worsted weight; 100% pure wool; 210 yds/100g per ball): 1 ball each navy #10 (A), white #8 (B) and red #150 (C)
- Size 6 (4mm) needles
- Size 7 (4.5mm) needles or size needed to obtain gauge
- Tapestry needle
- 3 (½-inch) buttons
- 11 inches (⅛-inch-wide) elastic, slightly stretched

Gauge

20 sts and 28 sts = 4 inches/10cm in St st with larger needles.
To save time, take time to check gauge.

Special Abbreviation

Make 1 (M1): Insert LH needle from front to back into strand between st just worked and next st, k1-tbl.

Pattern Note

When changing color bring new color under and around previous color to avoid holes.

Sweater

Back

With smaller needles and C, cast on 34 sts.
Knit 3 rows.

Change to larger needles.

Next row: With A, k17; with B, k17.

Continue in St st in color pat as established until piece measures 6½ inches, making sure to twist colors on WS. Bind off loosely.

Front

Work as for back until piece measures 5 inches, ending by working a WS row.

Shape neck

K14 sts, bind off center 6 sts, knit to end.

Dec 1 st at each neck edge [every row] 3 times—11 sts each side.

Work even until piece measures 6½ inches. Bind off loosely.

Shoulder buttonhole band

Sew right shoulder seam.

With RS of left front shoulder facing, smaller needles and C, pick up and knit 11 sts along shoulder. Knit 1 row.

Next row (buttonhole row): K3, [yo, k2tog, k2] twice.

Knit 1 row. Bind off loosely.

Shoulder button band

With RS of left back shoulder facing, smaller needles and C, pick up 11 sts along shoulder beg in 7th st from center.

Knit 3 rows. Bind off loosely.

Neckband

With RS of front facing, smaller needles and C, beg at the top of button band, pick up and knit 37 sts around neck edge to back band.

Knit 1 row.

Next row (RS): K1, yo, k2tog, knit to end.

Knit 1 row. Bind off loosely.

Sleeves

With smaller needles and C, cast on 21 sts. Knit 3 rows.

Change to larger needles.

Beg with knit row and B work in St st, alternating 2 rows B and 2 rows A, and *at the same time* inc 1 st each side [every 4th row] 3 times—27 sts.

Work even in pat until piece measures 3½ inches. Bind off loosely.

Assembly

Mark 2½ inches down from shoulder on each side. Sew sleeves between markers. Sew side and sleeve seams. Sew buttons opposite to button holes, having 2 buttons on shoulder band and 1 button on back neckband.

Shorts

Left side

Beg at waist, with larger needles and A, cast on 31 sts.

Beg with knit (RS) row work 4 rows in St st.

Next row (turning ridge): Purl.

Continue in St st until piece measures 2 inches, ending with a WS row.

Inc row (RS): Knit to last st, M1 (back seam), k1.

Hat

Garter band

With smaller needles and B, cast on 58 sts. Work in garter st for 12 rows.

Change to larger needles. Beg with knit row, work in St st for 6 rows.

Crown

Row 1: K1, [k6, k2tog] 7 times, k1—51 sts.

Row 2 and all even numbered rows: Purl.

Rep Inc row [every 4th row] 3 times more—35 st.

Work even until piece measures 4½ inches, ending with a RS row.

Next row (WS): Bind off 2 sts (back), purl across.

Next row (RS): Knit.

Next row: Bind off 2 sts, purl across.

Work even until piece measures 6 inches, ending with a RS row.

Knit 3 rows. Bind off loosely.

Right side

Work as for Left side until piece measures 2 inches, ending by working a WS row.

Inc row (RS): K1, M1 (back seam), knit to end.

Rep Inc row [every 4th row] 3 times more—35 sts.

Work even until piece measures 4½ inches, ending with a WS row.

Next row (RS): Bind off 2 sts (back), knit across.

Next row: Purl.

Next row: Bind off 2 sts, knit across.

Work even until piece measures 6 inches, ending with a RS row.

Knit 3 rows. Bind off loosely.

Assembly

Sew back seam of left and right sides tog from waist to the bound-off sts. Sew the front seam of left and right sides tog to the same place as back. Sew each leg tog. Sew piece of elastic tog to form a ring. Fold waist edge on turning ridge and sew the band in place over the elastic.

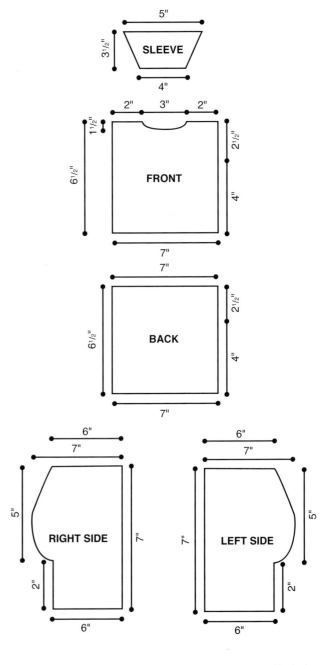

Row 3: K1, [k5, k2tog] 7 times, k1—44 sts.

Row 5: K1 [k4, k2tog] 7 times, k1—37 sts.

Row 7: K1, [k3, k2tog] 7 times, k1—30 sts.

Row 9: K1, [k2, k2tog] 7 times, k1—23 sts.

Row 11: K1, [k1, k2tog] 7 times, k1—16 sts.

Row 13: K1, [k2tog] 7 times, end k1—9 sts.

Cut yarn leaving 6-inch tail. Thread yarn into tapestry needle, draw yarn through sts, pulling tightly to close. Sew seam. ❖

Casual Caitlyn

Designs by Andra Knight-Bowman

Skill Level

■■■□ INTERMEDIATE

Finished Measurements

Chest: 14 inches
Sweater length: 7 inches, including lower border
Pant length: 10 inches

Materials

- Plymouth Baby Alpaca Worsted (worsted weight; 100% baby alpaca; 102 yds/50g per skein): 2 skeins each beige #100 (MC) and charcoal #813 (CC)
- Size 7 (4.5mm) needles or size needed to obtain gauge
- Tapestry needle
- 11 inches (⅛-inch-wide) elastic, slightly stretched

Gauge

20 sts and 28 rows = 4 inches/10cm in St st.
To save time, take time to check gauge.

Special Abbreviation

Make 1 (M1): Insert LH needle from front to back into strand between st just worked and next st, k1-tbl.

Pattern Notes

The sweater in made in Main Color (MC); pants are made in Contrasting Color (CC).

Body of sweater is made in 4 pieces; left and right back, and left and right front that mirror each other. The pieces are seamed down the middle.

Use thumb cast-on throughout entire sweater (for thumb cast-on instructions see page 14).

Slip the first stitch of every row purlwise with yarn in front then take yarn to back between needles.

Sweater

Left Back

Step 1
With MC, cast on 35 sts.

Row 1 (RS): Sl 1, knit to end. Mark as RS row.

Row 2: Sl 1, k15, k3tog, k16.

Row 3: Sl 1, knit to end.

Row 4: Sl 1, k14, k3tog, k15.

Row 5: Sl 1, knit to end.

Continue in this manner, having 1 less st on each side of dec until 3 sts rem. K3tog. Turn to RS.

Step 2
Row 1 (RS): Working in each ridge across top edge, pick up and knit 13 sts, leaving last 3 ridges unworked for armhole; cast on 13 sts—27 sts (includes st on needle at end of Step 1).

Row 2: Sl 1, k11, k3tog, k12.

Row 3: Sl 1, knit to end.

Row 4: Sl 1, k10, k3tog, k11.

Row 5: Sl 1, knit to end.

Continue in this manner, having 1 less st on each side of dec until 3 sts rem. K3tog. Fasten off.

Right Back

Step 1
Work Step 1 as for left back. Fasten off.

Step 2
Row 1 (RS): With RS facing, turn block one quarter turn to the left. Cast-on edge will be at right and bottom of block (a mirror image of left back).

Cast on 13 sts. Leaving first 3 ridges at top of block unworked for armhole, beg in next ridge to pick up and knit 14 sts—27 sts.

Row 2: Sl 1, k11, k3tog, k12.

Row 3: Sl 1, knit to end.

Row 4: Sl 1, k10, k3tog, k11.

Row 5: Sl 1, knit to end.

Continue in this manner, having 1 less st on each side of dec until 3 sts rem. K3tog. Fasten off.

Right Front
Work as for left back.

Left Front
Work as for right back.

Assembly
Sew left and right back pieces tog at center back. Sew left and right front pieces tog at center front, leaving 2 inches open for neck. Sew front and back shoulders tog for 1-inch shoulder seam.

Sleeves
With RS facing, pick up and knit 24 sts along inside of armhole edge (do not pick up along unworked underarm ridges).

Row 1: Sl 1, knit to end.

Rep Row 1 until sleeve measures 5½ inches. Bind off loosely.

Collar
With WS facing (this becomes the RS of collar), beg at center front, pick up and knit 1 st in each ridge around neck opening.

Thumb Method Cast-On

With yarn, make a slip knot on needle. Wrap yarn around thumb.

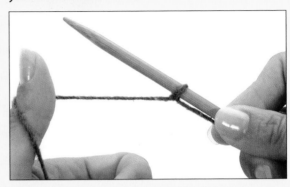

Slide needle through loop on thumb.

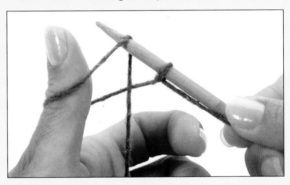

Repeat until desired number of sts are on needle.

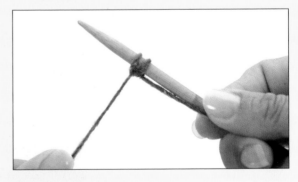

Row 1: Sl 1, knit to end.

Rep Row 1 until collar measures 1 inch. Bind off loosely.

Lower Borders
With RS facing, pick up and knit 1 st in each st across back.

Row 1: Sl 1, knit to end.

Rep Row 1 until border measures 1 inch. Bind off loosely.

Rep for front.

Finishing

Sew armhole edge to sleeve. Sew sleeve seam reversing seam on lower edge for cuff. Sew side seams, leaving lower border open at bottom. Fold back bottom of sleeve for cuff.

Pants

Left side

Beg at waist, with larger needles and CC, cast on 31 sts.

Beg with knit (RS) row, work 4 rows in St st.

Next row (RS): Purl across for turning ridge.

Beg with purl row, work in St st until piece measures 2 inches, ending with a WS row.

Inc row (RS): Knit to last st, M1 (back seam), k1.

Rep Inc row [every 4th row] 3 times—35 st.

Work even until piece measures 4½ inches, ending with a RS row.

Next row (WS): Bind off 2 sts (back), purl across.

Next row (RS): Knit.

Next row: Bind off 2 sts, purl across.

Work even until piece measures 10 inches, ending with a RS row.

Work 6 rows of rev St st. Bind off loosely.

Right side

Work as for Left side until piece measures 2 inches, ending with a WS row.

Inc row (RS): Knit 1, M1 (back seam), knit across.

Rep Inc row [every 4th row] 3 times—35 sts.

Work even until piece measures 4½ inches, ending with a WS row.

Next row (RS): Bind off 2 sts (back), knit across.

Next row: Purl.

Next row: Bind off 2 sts, knit across.

Work even until piece measures 10 inches, ending by working a RS row.

Work 6 rows of rev St st. Bind off loosely.

Assembly

Sew back seam of left and right sides tog from waist to the bind off sts. Sew the front seam of left and right sides tog to the same place as back. Sew each leg tog. Sew piece of elastic tog to form a ring. Fold the top band down on turning ridge and sew the band in place over the elastic. Fold up lower edge of pant legs for cuff. ❖

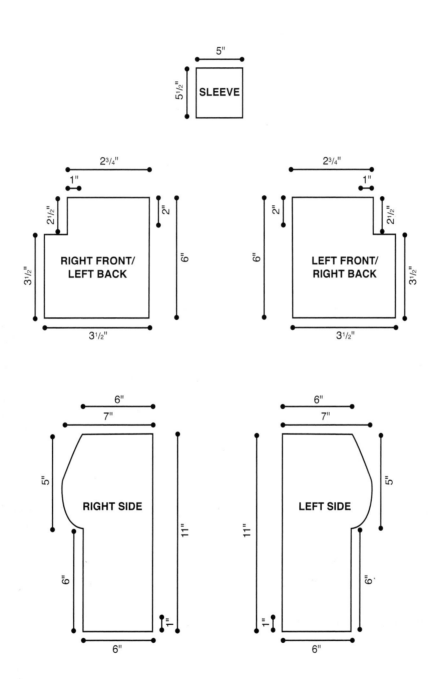

Evening-Wear Ella

Design by Andra Knight-Bowman

Skill Level
◼◼◻◻ EASY

Finished Measurements
Chest: 11 inches
Length: 10½ inches

Materials
- Plymouth Gold Rush (fingering weight; 80% viscose/20% metallised polyester; 109 yds/25g per cone): 3 cones purple #85
- Size 5 (3.75mm) needles
- Size 6 (4mm) needles or size needed to obtain gauge
- Cable needle
- Tapestry needle

Gauge
25 sts and 32 rows = 4 inches/10cm in St st with larger needles.
To save time, take time to check gauge.

Back
With smaller needles, cast on 41 sts. Knit 3 rows.

Change to larger needles and work in St st for 9¼ inches, ending with a WS row.

Change to smaller needles

Next row (RS): K4 [k2tog, k4] 6 times, end k1—35 sts.

Knit 3 rows.

Work 7 rows in St st.

Knit 3 rows. Bind off loosely.

Front
With smaller needles, cast on 51 sts. Knit 3 rows. Change to larger needles and work in St st for 9¼ inches, ending with a WS row.

Change to smaller needles.

Next row (RS): [K2tog, k3] 3 times, sl next 5 sts onto cn, hold in front, knit next 5 sts, one at a time tog with sts on cn, k1, sl next 5 sts onto cn, hold in back, knit next 5 sts, one at a time tog with st on cn, [k2tog, k3] 3 times—35 sts.

Knit 3 rows.

Work 4 rows in St st.

Eyelet opening (RS): K16, yo, k3tog, yo, k16 sts—35 sts.

Work 2 more row of St st.

Knit 3 rows. Bind off loosely

Scarf

With larger needles, cast on 6 sts. Work in garter st for 22 inches. Bind off loosely.

Assembly

Sew side seams. Thread each end of scarf through eyelet holes from back to front around neck. Tie in knot over eyelet opening at center front. ❖

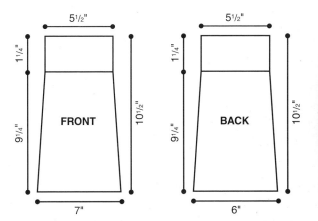

FRONT
5½"
1¼"
9¼"
10½"
7"

BACK
5½"
1¼"
9¼"
10½"
6"

House of White Birches, Berne, Indiana 46711   DRGnetwork.com

Jogging Josie

Designs by Andra Knight-Bowman

Skill Level

◼◼◼◻ INTERMEDIATE

Finished Measurements

Chest: 14 inches
Shirt Length: 6½ inches
Pant Length: 9½ inches

Materials

- Plymouth Jeannee Worsted (worsted weight; 51% cotton/49% acrylic; 110 yds/50g per ball): 3 balls gray #1 (MC) and 1 ball pink #4 (CC)
- Size 5 (3.75mm) needles
- Size 7 (4.5mm) needles or size needed to obtain gauge
- Size E/4 (3.5mm) crochet hook
- Stitch holder
- Tapestry needle

Gauge

20 sts and 28 rows = 4 inches/10cm in St st with larger needles.
To save time, take time to check gauge.

Special Abbreviation

Make 1 (M1): Insert LH needle from front to back into strand between st just worked and next st, k1-tbl.

Sweatshirt

Back

With MC and smaller needles, cast on 35 sts.

Row 1: *K1, p1; rep from * to last st, k1.

Row 2: *P1, k1; rep from * to last st, p1.

Rep [Rows 1 and 2] twice. Rep Row 1.

Change to larger needles and work in St st for 6½ inches. Bind off loosely.

Front

Work as for back until piece measures 4 inches, ending with a WS row.

Shape neck

Work 17 sts, attach 2nd ball of yarn, bind off center st, work to end. Working both sides at once with separate balls of yarn, continue in St st until piece measures 6½ inches, ending with a WS row.

Shape shoulders

Bind off 10 sts, place next 7 sts on holder; place 7 sts on holder, bind off rem 10 sts.

Sleeves

With MC and smaller needles, cast on 21 sts. Work rib as for back.

Change to larger needles and work in St st inc 1 st each side [every 4th row] 3 times—27 sts.

Continue even in St st until piece measures 3½ inches. Bind off loosely.

Sew shoulder seams.

Hood

With RS facing, larger needles and MC, attach yarn and knit 7 sts at right front neck from holder, pick up 18 sts across back neck edge, knit rem 7 sts for left front neck from holder—32 sts.

Continue in St st for 3 rows.

Inc row (RS): K15, M1, k2, M1, k15—34 sts.

Work 3 rows even.

Inc row: K16, M1, k2, M1, k16—36 sts.

Work 3 rows even.

Inc row: K17, M1, k2, M1, k17—38 sts.

Work 3 rows even.

Inc row: K18, M1, k2, M1, k18—40 sts.

Work even in St st until hood measures 4 inches, ending with a WS row.

Dec row (RS): K17, k2tog, k2, ssk, k17—38 sts.

Work 1 row.

Dec row: K16, k2tog, k2, ssk, k16—36 sts.

Work 1 row.

Dec row: K15, k2tog, k2, ssk, k15—34 sts.

Work 1 row.

Dec row: K14, k2tog, k2, ssk, k14—32 sts.

Work 1 row. Bind off loosely.

Pocket

With MC and larger needles, cast on 19 sts. Work in St st for 2 rows.

Next row (RS): K1, ssk, knit to last 3 sts, k2tog, k1—17 sts.

Next row: Purl.

Rep [last 2 rows] 3 times—11 sts. Bind off loosely.

Assembly

Mark 2½ inches from shoulder on each edge. Sew sleeves between markers. Sew side and sleeve seams. Sew the top of hood tog. With CC, work 1 rnd of sc around hood and pocket. Referring to photo, center pocket on front and sew in place leaving sides of pocket open.

Sweatpants

Left side

Beg at waist with larger needle and MC, cast on 31 sts. Work in St st for 4 rows.

Next row (RS): Purl for turning ridge.

Next row: P14 MC, p1 CC, p1 MC, p1 CC, p14 MC.

Next row: K14 MC, k1 CC, k1 MC, k1 CC, k14 MC.

Next row: P14 MC, p1 CC, p1 MC, p1 CC, p14 MC.

Drawstring opening: K2, yo, k2tog, work in pat across.

Continue even in pat until piece measures 2 inches, ending with a WS row.

Inc row (RS): Work in pat to last st, M1 (back seam), k1.

Rep Inc row [every 4th row] 3 times—35 st.

Work even in pat until piece measures 4½ inches, ending with a RS row.

Next row (WS): Bind off 2 sts (back), work in pat across.

Next row (RS): Work in pat across.

Next row: Bind off 2 sts, work in pat across.

Work even until piece measures 9½ inches, ending with a WS row. Bind off loosely.

Right side

Work as for left side to drawstring opening.

Drawstring opening: Knit to last 4 sts, k2tog, yo, k2.

Work even in pat until piece measures 2 inches, ending with a WS row.

Inc row (RS): Knit 1, M1 (back seam), work in pat across.

Rep Inc row [every 4th row] 3 times—35 sts.

Work even in pat until piece measures 4½ inches, ending with a WS row.

Next row (RS): Bind off 2 sts (back), work in pat across.

Next row: Work in pat across.

Next row: Bind off 2 sts, work in pat across.

Work even until piece measures 9½ inches, ending with a WS row. Bind off loosely.

Assembly

Sew back seam of left and right sides tog to the bind off sts. Sew the front seam of left and right sides tog to the same place as back. Sew each leg tog. With crochet hook and CC, chain for 20 inches. Fold waist edge on turning ridge and to make casing for chain, pulling ends of chain through eyelet openings. Sew the band in place over chain. ❖

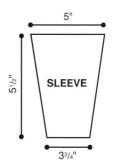

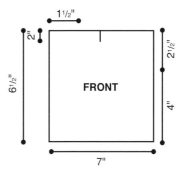

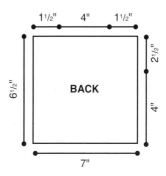

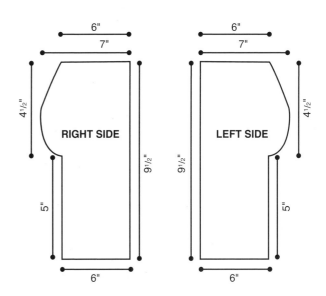

House of White Birches, Berne, Indiana 46711   DRGnetwork.com

Nighttime Nicole

Designs by Andra Knight-Bowman

Skill Level

◼◼◼▢ INTERMEDIATE

Finished Measurements

Chest: 11 inches
Length: 8½ inches

Materials

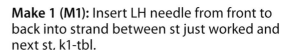

- Plymouth Dreambaby Shine (DK weight yarn; 45% microfiber acrylic/45% nylon/10% rayon; 160 yds/50g per ball): 2 balls white #100
- Size 6 (4mm) needles or size needed to obtain gauge
- Size E/4 (3.5mm) crochet hook
- Tapestry needle
- 11 inches ⅛-inch-wide elastic, slightly stretched
- 1 yard ½-inch-wide ribbon

Gauge

22 sts and 28 rows = 4 inches/10cm in St st.
To save time, take time to check gauge.

Special abbreviations

Knit in front and back (kfb): Knit in front and back of next st to inc 1 st.

Make 1 (M1): Insert LH needle from front to back into strand between st just worked and next st, k1-tbl.

Top

Back and Front

Make 2 alike

Cast on 67 sts.

Next row (WS): Purl.

Beg with knit row, work 6 rows in St st.

Next row (RS): *K1, k2tog; rep from * to last st, k1—45 sts.

Next row: Knit.

Beg Eyelet pat

Row 1 (RS): Knit.

Row 2 and all even-numbered rows: Purl.

Row 3: K1, *yo, k2tog, k2; rep from * across.

Row 5: Knit.

Row 7: K3, *yo, k2tog, k2; rep from * to last 3 sts, yo, k2tog.

Row 8: Purl.

Rep Rows 1–8 until piece measures 5 inches, ending with a WS row.

Next row (RS): *K1, k2tog; rep from * across—30 sts.

House of White Birches, Berne, Indiana 46711

Next row (WS): Knit.

Beg with knit row work 4 rows in St st.

Shape armhole
Bind off 7 sts at beg of next 2 rows—16 sts.

Work 4 rows even.

Shape neck
Next row (RS): K4, join new ball of yarn and bind off center 8 sts, k4.

Single Crochet (sc)
Insert the hook in the second chain through the center of the V. Bring the yarn over the hook from back to front.

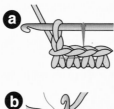

Draw the yarn through the chain stitch and onto the hook.

Again bring yarn over the hook from back to front and draw it through both loops on hook.

For additional rows of single crochet, insert the hook under both loops of the previous stitch instead of through the center of the V as when working into the chain stitch.

Reverse Single Crochet (reverse sc)
Ch 1 (a). Skip first st. Working from left to right, insert hook in next st from front to back (b), draw up lp on hook, yo, and draw through both lps on hook (c).

Continue in St st working both sides at once with separate balls of yarn until armhole measures 2½ inches. Bind off loosely.

Sew shoulder seams.

Armhole ruffle
With RS facing attach yarn at inside of armhole, pick up and knit 29 sts around armhole edge, turn. Knit 1 row.

Next row (RS) *K1, kfb; rep from * to last st, k1—43 sts.

Beg with purl row, work 3 rows in St st. Bind off loosely.

Assembly
Sew side seams.

Join yarn at one shoulder seam, work 1 rnd of sc around neck opening. Do not turn. Working from left to right work 1 rnd of reverse sc around, join. Finish off.

Tie ribbon around waist, if desired.

Panties
Back
Note: Panties are made in one piece beg at back waist and ending at front waist.

Beg at back waist, cast on 34 sts.

Beg with knit row work 4 rows in St st.

Next row (RS): Purl for turning ridge.

Beg with purl row work 7 rows in St st.

Inc row (RS): K1, M1, knit to last st, M1, k1—36 sts.

Rep Inc row [every 4th row] twice more—40 sts.

Work even until piece measures 3 inches, ending with a WS row.

Bind off 6 sts at beg of next 2 rows. Dec 1 st each side [every row] 5 times, then [every other row] 5 times—8 sts.

Front
Cast-on 2 sts at beg of next 4 rows—16 sts.

Cast-on 3 sts at beg of next 4 rows—28 sts.

Cast-on 5 sts at beg of next 2 rows—38 sts.

Dec 1 st each side [every 4th row] 3 times—32 sts.

30

Work even until piece measures 2½ inches from front leg opening, ending with a WS row.

Next row (RS): Purl for turning ridge.

Beg with purl row work 4 rows of St st. Bind off loosely.

Assembly
Sew side seams.

Work 1 rnd of sc around leg opening. Do not turn. Working from left to right, work 1 rnd of reverse sc. Fasten off.

Sew elastic tog to form a ring. Fold the top band down on turning ridge and sew in place over the elastic. ❖

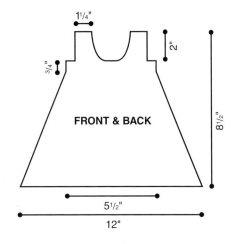

1¼"

2"

¾"

8½"

FRONT & BACK

5½"

12"

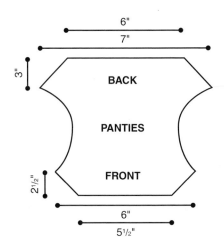

6"

7"

3"

BACK

PANTIES

FRONT

2½"

6"

5½"

Rah-Rah Rachel

Designs by Andra Knight-Bowman

Skill Level

■■■□ INTERMEDIATE

Finished Measurements

Chest: 14 inches
Sweater length: 6½ inches
Skirt length: 4½ inches

Materials

- Plymouth Encore Worsted (worsted weight; 75% acrylic/25% wool; 200 yds/100g per ball): 1 ball each orange #1014 (MC) and purple #1034 (CC)
- Size 7 (4.5mm) needles
- Size 8 (5mm) needles or size needed to obtain gauge
- Stitch holder
- Tapestry needle
- 11 inches (⅛-inch-wide) elastic, slightly stretched

Gauge

18 sts and 25 rows = 4 inches/10cm in St st with larger needles.
To save time, take time to check gauge.

Sweater

Back

With CC and smaller needles, cast on 31 sts.

Row 1 (WS): Knit.

Rows 2 (RS) and 3: With MC, knit.

Rows 4 and 5: With CC, knit.

Change to MC and larger needles. Work in St st for 6½ inches, ending with a WS row. Bind off loosely.

Front

Work as for back until piece measures 3½ inches, ending with a WS row.

Shape neck

Work 15 sts, place center st on holder, work rem 15 sts. Work 1 row.

Dec 1 st each neck edge [every other row] 6 times—9 sts on each side.

Continue even until piece measures 6½ inches, ending with a WS row. Bind off loosely.

Sleeves

With CC and smaller needles, cast on 17 sts.

Row 1 (WS): Knit.

Rows 2 (RS) and 3: With MC, knit.

Rows 4 and 5: With CC, knit.

Change to MC and larger needles. Work in St st, inc 1 st each side [every 4th row] 3 times—23 sts.

Continue even in pat until piece measures 3½ inches. Bind off loosely.

Neckband

Sew right shoulders tog.

With RS facing, CC and smaller needles and starting at left front shoulder, pick up and knit 16 sts to center st on holder, place marker, knit center st from holder, place marker, pick up and knit 16 sts to right shoulder, pick up and knit 13 sts across back neck, turn.

Next row: Knit.

Dec row: With MC, knit to 2 sts before marker, k2tog, k1, k2tog, knit to end.

Next row: Knit.

With CC, rep Dec row. Bind off loosely.

Assembly

With CC, work desired letter in duplicate st in center of front *(see duplicate instructions on page 34).*

Mark 2½ inches from shoulder on each side and sew sleeves in place between markers. Sew side and sleeve seams. Weave in ends.

Skirt

Back/Front

Make 2 alike

Beg at lower edge with CC and smaller needles, cast on 37 sts.

Row 1 (WS): Knit.

Rows 2 (RS) and 3: With MC, knit.

Rows 4 and 5: With CC, knit.

Change to larger needles and work in St st for 3½ inches, ending with a WS row.

Next row (RS): *K1, k2tog; rep from * to last st, end k1—25 sts.

Waist casing

Next row (WS): Knit.

Next row (RS): Knit.

Next row: Purl.

Rep last 2 rows once more.

Next row (RS): Purl (turning ridge).

Next row (WS): Purl.

Next row: Knit.

Next row: Purl.

Bind off loosely.

Assembly

Sew side seams. Sew elastic tog to form a ring. Fold the top band down on turning ridge and sew in place over the elastic.

Using MC and CC, make 2 (2-inch) pompoms *(See pompom instructions on page 34).* ❖

Pompoms

Cut two cardboard circles in size specified in pattern. Cut a hole in the center of each circle, about ½ inch in diameter. Thread a tapestry needle with a length of yarn doubled. Holding both circles together, insert needle through center hole, over the outside edge, through center again (Fig. 1) until entire circle is covered and center hole is filled (thread more length of yarn as needed).

With sharp scissors, cut yarn between the two circles all around the circumference (Fig. 2).

Using two 12-inch strands of yarn, slip yarn between circles and overlap yarn ends two or three times (Fig. 3) to prevent knot from slipping, pull tightly and tie into a firm knot. Remove cardboard and fluff out pompom by rolling it between your hands. Trim even with scissors, leaving tying ends for attaching pompom to project.

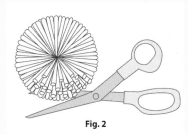

Fig. 1

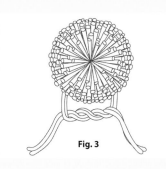

Fig. 2

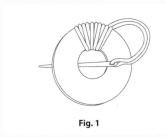

Fig. 3

Duplicate Stitch

From underneath piece, bring yarn up in the center of the stitch below the stitch to be duplicated. Place needle from right to left behind both sides of the stitch above the one being duplicated, and pull yarn through (a). Complete the stitch by returning the needle to where you began (b).

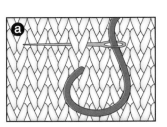

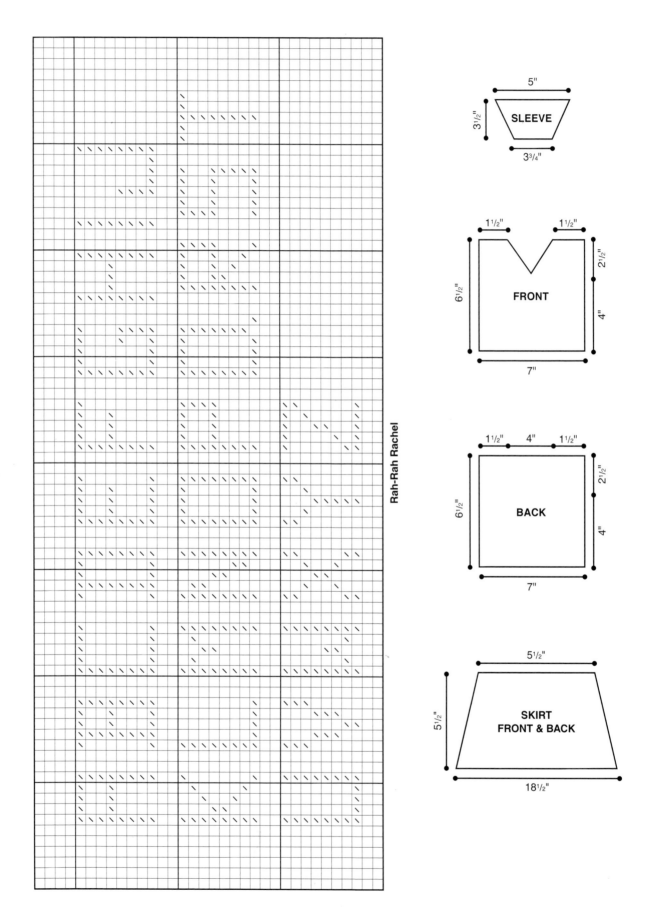

Rah-Rah Rachel

SLEEVE

5"

3½"

3¾"

FRONT

1½"   1½"

6½"

2½"

4"

7"

BACK

1½"   4"   1½"

6½"

2½"

4"

7"

SKIRT
FRONT & BACK

5½"

5½"

18½"

Bathtime Betsy

Designs by Andra Knight-Bowman

Skill Level

 EASY

Finished Measurements

Chest: 14 inches
Length: 11 inches

Materials

- Plymouth Oh My! (bulky weight; 100% nylon; 70 yds/50g per ball): 3 balls pink #54
- Size 9 (5.5mm) needles or size needed to obtain gauge
- Stitch markers
- Stitch holders
- Tapestry needle

5 BULKY

Gauge

16 sts and 24 rows = 4 inches/10cm in St st.
To save time, take time to check gauge.

Robe

Body

Cast on 56 sts. Work 8 rows in garter st.

Row 1 (RS): Knit 5, place marker, k10 (right front), place marker, k26 (back), place marker, k10, place marker, k5 (left front).

Row 2 (WS): Knit 5, purl to last marker, k5.

Continue in established pat working the first and last 5 sts in garter st and center sts in St st until body measures 8 inches, ending with a WS row.

Shape Right Front neck & armhole

Dec row: Knit to first marker, ssk, knit to 2nd marker, turn.

Work 1 row in established pat.

Rep Dec row [every other row] 3 times—11 sts.

Work even until piece measures 11 inches, ending with a WS row. Place 5 garter sts on holder, bind off rem sts.

Shape Back

With RS facing, join yarn and k26 sts for back. Work in St st until piece measure 11 inches, ending with a WS row. Bind off loosely.

Shape Left Front neck & armhole

Dec row: With RS facing, join yarn and work across left front to 2 sts before marker, k2tog, knit to end.

Work 1 row in established pat.

Rep Dec row [every other row] 3 times more—11 sts.

Work even until piece measures 11 inches, ending with a WS row.

Collar

Next row (RS): Bind off 6 sts, knit rem sts.

Work in garter st on rem 5 sts for 2¾ inches. Bind off.

Place sts from holder at right front on needle, attach yarn, work in garter st for 2¾ inches. Bind off.

Sleeves

Cast on 16 sts. Work 8 rows in garter st.

Work in St st, inc 1 st each side [every other row] 4 times. Work even until piece measures 3½ inches. Bind off loosely.

Belt

Cast on 4 sts. Work in garter st for 32 inches. Bind off.

Assembly

Sew shoulders tog. Sew collar tog at the bound-off edges, then sew in place along back neck edge. Sew in sleeves. Sew sleeve seams.

Slippers

Beg at center back, cast on 15 sts.

Row 1 (WS): K4, p1, k5, p1, k4 sts.

Row 2 (RS): Knit.

Rows 3–10: Rep [Rows 1 and 2] 4 times.

Row 11: *P1, k1; rep from * to last st, p1.

Row 12: *K1, p1; rep from * to last st, k1.

Rows 13–18: Rep [Rows 11 and 12] 3 times.

Row 19: Rep Row 11.

Cut yarn, leaving 6-inch tail. Thread tail into tapestry needle and draw yarn through sts on needle, pulling tightly. Sew ends of rib section tog for top of foot. Fold the cast on edge in half and sew tog for back seam.

Make 2 (1-inch) pompoms and attach to slippers. *(See pompom instructions on page 34).* ❖

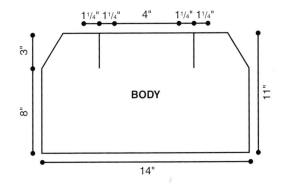

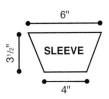

Standard Abbreviations

[ ]work instructions within brackets as many times as directed

( )work instructions within parentheses in the place directed

**repeat instructions following the asterisks as directed

* repeat instructions following the single asterisk as directed

" inch(es)

approx approximately

beg begin/beginning

CC contrasting color

ch chain stitch

cm centimeter(s)

cn cable needle

dec decrease/decreases/ decreasing

dpn(s) double-point needle(s)

g gram

inc increase/increases/increasing

k knit

k2tog knit 2 stitches together

LH left hand

lp(s) loop(s)

m meter(s)

M1 make one stitch

MC main color

mm millimeter(s)

oz ounce(s)

p purl

pat(s) pattern(s)

p2tog purl 2 stitches together

psso pass slipped stitch over

p2sso pass 2 slipped stitches over

rem remain/remaining

rep repeat(s)

rev St st reverse stockinette stitch

RH right hand

rnd(s) rounds

RS right side

skp slip, knit, pass stitch over— one stitch decreased

sk2p slip 1, knit 2 together, pass slip stitch over the knit 2 together—2 stitches have been decreased

sl slip

sl 1k slip 1 knitwise

sl 1p slip 1 purlwise

sl st slip stitch(es)

ssk slip, slip, knit these 2 stitches together—a decrease

st(s) stitch(es)

St st stockinette stitch/ stocking stitch

tbl through back loop(s)

tog together

WS wrong side

wyib with yarn in back

wyif with yarn in front

yd(s) yard(s)

yfwd yarn forward

yo yarn over

House of White Birches, Berne, Indiana 46711   DRGnetwork.com

Knitting Basics

Cast On

Leaving an end about an inch long for each stitch to be cast on, make a slip knot on the right needle.

Place the thumb and index finger of your left hand between the yarn ends with the long yarn end over your thumb, and the strand from the skein over your index finger. Close your other fingers over the strands to hold them against your palm. Spread your thumb and index fingers apart and draw the yarn into a "V."

Place the needle in front of the strand around your thumb and bring it underneath this strand. Carry the needle over and under the strand on your index finger.

Draw through loop on thumb.

Drop the loop from your thumb and draw up the strand to form a stitch on the needle.

Repeat until you have cast on the number of stitches indicated in the pattern. Remember to count the beginning slip knot as a stitch.

Cable Cast-On

This type of cast on is used when adding stitches in the middle or at the end of a row.

Make a slip knot on the left needle. Knit a stitch in this knot and place it on the left needle. Insert the right needle between the last two stitches on the left needle. Knit a stitch and place it on the left needle. Repeat for each stitch needed.

Knit (k)

Insert tip of right needle from front to back in next stitch on left needle.

Bring yarn under and over the tip of the right needle.

Pull yarn loop through the stitch with right needle point.

Slide the stitch off the left needle. The new stitch is on the right needle.

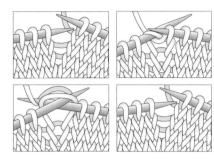

Purl (p)

With yarn in front, insert tip of right needle from back to front through next stitch on the left needle.

Bring yarn around the right needle counterclockwise. With right needle, draw yarn back through the stitch.

Slide the stitch off the left needle. The new stitch is on the right needle.

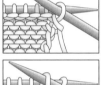

Bind-Off

Binding off (knit)

Knit first two stitches on left needle. Insert tip of left needle into first stitch worked on right needle and pull it over the second stitch and completely off the needle.

Knit the next stitch and repeat. When one stitch remains on right needle, cut yarn and draw tail through last stitch to fasten off.

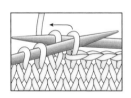

Binding off (purl)

Purl first two stitches on left needle. Insert tip of left needle into first stitch worked on right needle and pull it over the second stitch and completely off the needle.

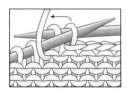

Purl the next stitch and repeat. When one stitch remains on right needle, cut yarn and draw tail through last stitch to fasten off.

Increase (inc)

Two stitches in one stitch

Increase (knit)
Knit the next stitch in the usual manner, but don't remove the stitch from the left needle.
Place right needle behind left needle and knit again into the back of the same stitch. Slip original stitch off left needle.

Increase (purl)
Purl the next stitch in the usual manner, but don't remove the stitch from the left needle.
Place right needle behind left needle and purl again into the back of the same stitch. Slip original stitch off left needle.

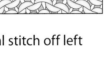

Invisible Increase (M1)
There are several ways to make or increase one stitch.

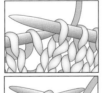

Make 1 with Left Twist (M1L)
Insert left needle from front to back under the horizontal loop between the last stitch worked and next stitch on left needle.

With right needle, knit into the back of this loop.

To make this increase on the purl side, insert left needle in same manner and purl into the back of the loop.

Make 1 with Right Twist (M1R)
Insert left needle from back to front under the horizontal loop between the last stitch worked and next stitch on left needle.

With right needle, knit into the front of this loop.

To make this increase on the purl side, insert left needle in same manner and purl into the front of the loop.

Make 1 with Backward Loop over the right needle
With your thumb, make a loop over the right needle.
Slip the loop from your thumb onto the needle and pull to tighten.

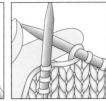

Make 1 in top of stitch below
Insert tip of right needle into the stitch on left needle one row below.

Knit this stitch, then knit the stitch on the left needle.

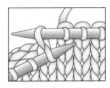

Decrease (dec)
Knit 2 together (k2tog)
Put tip of right needle through next two stitches on left needle as to knit. Knit these two stitches as one.

Purl 2 together (p2tog)
Put tip of right needle through next two stitches on left needle as to purl. Purl these two stitches as one.

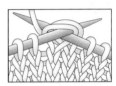

Slip, Slip, Knit (ssk)
Slip next two stitches, one at a time, as to knit from left needle to right needle.

Insert left needle in front of both stitches and work off needle together.

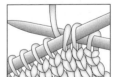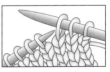

Slip, Slip, Purl (ssp)
Slip next two stitches, one at a time, as to knit from left needle to right needle. Slip these stitches back onto left needle keeping them twisted. Purl these two stitches together through back loops.

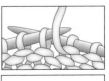

House of White Birches, Berne, Indiana 46711

Skill Levels

Beginner projects for first-time knitters using basic stitches. Minimal shaping.

Easy projects using basic stitches, repetitive stitch patterns, simple color changes, and simple shaping and finishing.

Intermediate projects with a variety of stitches, mid-level shaping and finishing.

Experienced projects using advanced techniques and stitches, detailed shaping and refined finishing.

Standard Yarn Weight System

Categories of yarn, gauge ranges, and recommended needle sizes

Yarn Weight Symbol & Category Names	1 SUPER FINE	2 FINE	3 LIGHT	4 MEDIUM	5 BULKY	6 SUPER BULKY
Type of Yarns in Category	Sock, Fingering, Baby	Sport, Baby	DK, Light Worsted	Worsted, Afghan, Aran	Chunky, Craft, Rug	Bulky, Roving
Knit Gauge Range* in Stockinette Stitch to 4 inches	27–32 sts	23–26 sts	21–24 sts	16–20 sts	12–15 sts	6–11 sts
Recommended Needle in Metric Size Range	2.25–3.25mm	3.25–3.75mm	3.75–4.5mm	4.5–5.5mm	5.5–8mm	8mm and larger
Recommended Needle U.S. Size Range	1 to 3	3 to 5	5 to 7	7 to 9	9 to 11	11 and larger

* GUIDELINES ONLY: The above reflect the most commonly used gauges and needle sizes for specific yarn categories.

Basic Stitches

Garter Stitch

On straight needles knit every row. When working in the round on circular or double-point needles, knit one round then purl one round.

Stockinette Stitch

On straight needles knit right-side rows and purl wrong-side rows. When working on circular or double-point needles, knit all rounds.

Reverse Stockinette Stitch

On straight needles purl right-side rows and knit wrong-side rows. On circular or double-point needles, purl all rounds.

Ribbing

Combines knit and purl stitches within a row to give stretch to the garment. Ribbing is most often used for the lower edge of the front and back, the cuffs and neck edge of garments.

The rib pattern is established on the first row. On subsequent rows the knit stitches are knitted and purl stitches are purled to form the ribs.

Reading Pattern Instructions

Before beginning a pattern, look through it to make sure you are familiar with the abbreviations that are used.

Some patterns may be written for more than one size. In this case the smallest size is given first and others are placed in parentheses. When only one number is given, it applies to all sizes.

You may wish to highlight the numbers for the size you are making before beginning. It is also helpful to place a self-sticking note on the pattern to mark any changes made while working the pattern.

Measuring

To measure pieces, lay them flat on a smooth surface. Take the measurement in the middle of the piece. For example, measure the length to the armhole in the center of the front or back piece, not along the outer edge where the edges tend to curve or roll.

Gauge

The single most important factor in determining the finished size of a knit item is the gauge. Although not as important for flat, one-piece items, it is important when making a clothing item that needs to fit properly.

It is important to make a stitch-gauge swatch about 4 inches square with recommended patterns and needles before beginning.

Measure the swatch. If the number of stitches and rows are fewer than indicated under "Gauge" in the pattern, your needles are too large. Try another swatch with smaller-size needles. If the number of stitches and rows are more than indicated under "Gauge" in the pattern, your needles are too small. Try another swatch with larger-size needles.

Continue to adjust needles until correct gauge is achieved.

Working From Charts

When working with more than one color in a row, sometimes a chart is provided to follow the pattern. On the chart each square represents one stitch. A key is given indicating the color or stitch represented by each color or symbol in the box.

When working in rows, odd-numbered rows are usually read from right to left, and even-numbered rows from left to right.

Odd-numbered rows represent the right side of the work and are usually knit. Even-numbered rows represent the wrong side and are usually purled.

When working in rounds, every row on the chart is a right-side row, and is read from right to left.

Use of Zero

In patterns that include various sizes, zeros are sometimes necessary. For example, k0 (0,1) means if you are making the smallest or middle size, you would do nothing, and if you are making the largest size, you would k1.

Glossary

bind off—used to finish an edge

cast on—process of making foundation stitches used in knitting

decrease—means of reducing the number of stitches in a row

increase—means of adding to the number of stitches in a row

intarsia—method of knitting a multicolored pattern into the fabric

knitwise—insert needle into stitch as if to knit

make 1—method of increasing using the strand between the last stitch worked and the next stitch

place marker—placing a purchased marker or loop of contrasting yarn onto the needle for ease in working a pattern repeat

purlwise—insert needle into stitch as if to purl

right side—side of garment or piece that will be seen when worn

selvage stitch—edge stitch used to make seaming easier

slip, slip, knit—method of decreasing by moving stitches from left needle to right needle and working them together

slip stitch—an unworked stitch slipped from left needle to right needle, usually as if to purl

wrong side—side that will be inside when garment is worn

work even—continue to work in the pattern as established without working any increases or decreases

work in pattern as established—continue to work following the pattern stitch as it has been set up or established on the needle, working any increases or decreases in such a way that the established pattern remains the same

yarn over—method of increasing by wrapping the yarn over the right needle without working a stitch

House of White Birches, Berne, Indiana 46711

Photo Index

4

12

7

18

21

31

26

37

Knitting Needle Conversion Chart

U.S.	1	2	3	4	5	6	7	8	9	10	10½	11	13	15	17	19	35	50
Continental-mm	2.25	2.75	3.25	3.5	3.75	4	4.5	5	5.5	6	6.5	8	9	10	12.75	15	19	25

Inches into Millimetres & Centimetres

All measurements are rounded off slightly.

inches	mm	cm	inches	cm	inches	cm	inches	cm	inches	cm
⅛	3	0.3	3	7.5	13	33.0	26	66.0	39	99.0
¼	6	0.6	3½	9.0	14	35.5	27	68.5	40	101.5
⅜	10	1.0	4	10.0	15	38.0	28	71.0	41	104.0
½	13	1.3	4½	11.5	16	40.5	29	73.5	42	106.5
⅝	15	1.5	5	12.5	17	43.0	30	76.0	43	109.0
¾	20	2.0	5½	14	18	46.0	31	79.0	44	112.0
⅞	22	2.2	6	15.0	19	48.5	32	81.5	45	114.5
1	25	2.5	7	18.0	20	51.0	33	84.0	46	117.0
1¼	32	3.8	8	20.5	21	53.5	34	86.5	47	119.5
1½	38	3.8	9	23.0	22	56.0	35	89.0	48	122.0
1¾	45	4.5	10	25.5	23	58.5	36	91.5	49	124.5
2	50	5.0	11	28.0	24	61.0	37	94.0	50	127.0
2½	65	6.5	12	30.5	25	63.5	38	96.5		

HOUSE of WHITE BIRCHES
PUBLISHERS SINCE 1947

Fun-to-Knit Doll Clothes is published by DRG, 306 East Parr Road, Berne, IN 46711. Printed in USA. Copyright © 2009 DRG. All rights reserved. This publication may not be reproduced in part or in whole without written permission from the publisher.

RETAIL STORES: If you would like to carry this pattern book or any other DRG publications, visit DRGwholesale.com

Every effort has been made to ensure that the instructions in this publication are complete and accurate. We cannot, however, take responsibility for human error, typographical mistakes or variations in individual work. Please visit AnniesCustomerCare.com to check for pattern updates.

STAFF

Editor: Jeanne Stauffer
Assistant Editor: Erika Mann
Technical Editor: Kathy Wesley
Technical Artists: Nicole Gage, Pam Gregory
Copy Supervisor: Michelle Beck
Copy Editor: Amanda Ladig
Graphic Arts Supervisor: Ronda Bechinski

Graphic Artists: Erin Augsburger, Debby Keel
Art Director: Brad Snow
Assistant Art Director: Nick Pierce
Photography Supervisor: Tammy Christian
Photography: Matt Owen
Photo Stylist: Tammy Steiner

ISBN: 978-1-59217-277-1
4 5 6 7 8 9 10